HAPPY THANKSGIVING!

**OTHER BOOKS BY
CAROL BARKIN AND ELIZABETH JAMES**

How to Grow a Hundred Dollars

How to Keep a Secret:
Writing and Talking in Code

How to Write a Great School Report

How to Write a Term Paper

How to Write Your Best Book Report

The Scary Halloween Costume Book

What Do You Mean by "Average"?
Means, Medians, and Modes

HAPPY THANKSGIVING!

by Carol Barkin & Elizabeth James

Pictures by Giora Carmi

Lothrop, Lee & Shepard Books   New York

First Edition 1 2 3 4 5 6 7 8 9 10

Library of Congress Cataloging in Publication Data
Barkin, Carol. Happy Thanksgiving!
Summary: Discusses the significance of Thanksgiving, suggests various projects and activities for
celebrating it, and provides recipes for the holiday. 1. Thanksgiving cookery—Juvenile literature. 2.
Thanksgiving decorations—Juvenile literature. 3. Thanksgiving Day—Juvenile literature. [1.
Thanksgiving Day. 2. Thanksgiving cookery] I. James, Elizabeth. II. Carmi, Giora, ill. III. Title.
TX739.B33 1987   394.2′683   86-33734
ISBN 0-688-06800-6   ISBN 0-688-06801-4 (lib. bdg.)

THANKS!
to our families, who gave us lots to be grateful for,
and to Sue Alexander, a good friend

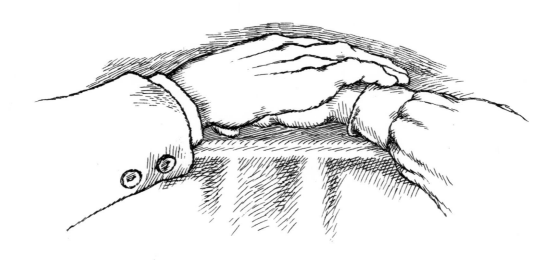

Contents

If April showers bring May flowers, what do May flowers bring?

The Pilgrims.

If the Pilgrims were alive today, what would they be most famous for?

Their age.

1. What Does Thanksgiving Really Mean?

If someone asked you what Thanksgiving was all about, you'd probably start telling the story of the Pilgrims and the Indians. Or you might describe the huge feast you had at your house last Thanksgiving. But a visitor from Mars might wonder why this holiday is called Thanksgiving. You haven't really explained what people are giving thanks for.

Of course, the Pilgrims were thankful that their tiny settlement had survived those first few perilous months in the New

World. They invited the Indians who had helped them plant and hunt to celebrate their first harvest—the food that would get them through another winter.

But these days most people living in the United States don't have to rely only on the food they grow themselves. Lots of different foods are available year-round in supermarkets and grocery stores. It's difficult to understand how it felt to know that a good harvest in the fall would make the difference between living and dying that winter.

Does this mean that Thanksgiving is just a way to remember a faraway part of our country's history and get a couple of days off from school? Sometimes it seems that the fourth Thursday in November is merely a day to pig out on turkey with all the trimmings and to watch football games on TV. Is this holiday really so meaningless for us today?

It needn't be. Since it was declared a national holiday more than one hundred years ago, Thanksgiving has traditionally been a family celebration. Perhaps some of your relatives travel every year to your house for the Thanksgiving weekend. It's fun to have cousins around to play with or grandparents who are thrilled to hear all about what you've been doing. Maybe your aunt is teaching you how to play the guitar or your grandpa helps you figure out how magic tricks work, and you realize how lucky you are. Or you might be secretly flattered that your little cousin thinks you're so wonderful he copies everything you do. There are lots of reasons to be thankful that you have such a great family.

When you start thinking about it, there are no doubt many things in your own life that make you happy. What about your best friend, who's always there to share your laughter and your tears? Maybe you have a great teacher this year who makes class exciting. Or perhaps your town has a terrific sports program for kids your age. These are things to remember on Thanksgiving Day.

But how will people know you feel thankful for the friendship or help they give you? How can you show your appreciation? Thanksgiving isn't traditionally a day for exchanging gifts, like Christmas or Chanukah, or for sending sentimental cards, like Valentine's Day. As a matter of fact, Thanksgiving traditions consist mainly of sharing a feast with family and friends and enjoying one another's company. Why not start some new family traditions that will be your own ways of giving thanks?

In this book you'll find ideas on how to create Thanksgiving customs for this year or for every year. Try out the ones that appeal to you or use these suggestions as starting points to come up with your own variations. Whether you carry out your Thanksgiving projects by yourself or get the whole family involved, you'll enjoy a holiday that you've helped to make special. So be creative and have a happy Thanksgiving!

11

Why can't you take a turkey to church?

Because it uses such fowl language.

What are the feathers on a turkey's wings called?

Turkey feathers.

2. Sharing the Thanksgiving Spirit

Almost from the beginning of Thanksgiving celebrations, people have shared their feast with those less fortunate than themselves. Looking forward to a table loaded with more food than they could eat often made people think about others who would not be sitting down to a plentiful dinner.

Maybe your family invites a neighbor who is all alone over for Thanksgiving. Or you might have helped pack up a basket of food to take to church to be distributed to the needy. Many organizations like churches, synagogues, community centers, and service clubs such as Rotary or Kiwanis give huge Thanksgiving dinners for people who have nowhere else to go.

Does your school or Scout troop collect cans of food to be put into Thanksgiving baskets? Some schools ask each student to bring in one can of any kind of food the week before Thanksgiving. It's a nice feeling to know that you've helped feed a hungry family with your donation, but you might also feel that you didn't actually do a lot. Asking Mom which extra can of soup or vegetables you can have and carrying it to school with you doesn't take much time or effort. How about taking this idea one step further?

You and a few friends can organize a food drive of your own at your local supermarket. First make sure you have a place to give the food you collect. Talk to the principal of your school or your minister or rabbi to arrange where the food is going to go and how it will get there. Then talk to the manager of the supermarket and explain what you want to do.

Here is an effective way to encourage grocery shoppers to donate food. Make a sign to hang from the front of a card table that you will set up near the store entrance. A big piece of cardboard that says ONE CAN HELPS FEED A FAMILY and a pyramid of food cans on the table will let shoppers know at a glance what's going on. As people approach the store, ask them if they will buy just one extra can of anything and give it to you when they leave. Be ready with suggestions. Thanksgiving foods like sweet potatoes or corn are fine, but so are other items like soups, juice, tuna fish, corned beef hash, or canned fruits and vegetables.

You will want to run your food drive either one or two Saturdays before Thanksgiving. It's a good idea to make your arrangements with the supermarket manager well in advance. When you go to ask the manager's permission to collect in front of the store, be sure to have all the information ready in your mind. Explain who you are, what you want to do, what organization the food will go to, and which adult will be helping you transport the cans of food at the end of the day. Maybe the manager will be willing to donate some grocery sacks or boxes to pack the food in.

The Saturday before Thanksgiving is a great time to ask for food donations at a market. People are likely to be in a giving mood. Besides, the cost of one can will be practically nothing compared to what they're spending on all the other food for the holiday. The reason you want people to donate food in cans instead of boxes or jars is that cans won't break or crush. And you won't have to worry about the food spoiling, the way you would with fresh meat or fruit.

What do you do when a nice person comes out with a cart packed to the brim and says, "Oh, no! I meant to get a can, but I forgot. Here's a dollar instead"? It's a good idea to prepare for this and to have an envelope to put the cash in. At the end of the day, use the money to buy more canned goods and add them to the collection.

You may be astonished at how much food you can collect this way. And you and your friends will feel really good about helping other people enjoy Thanksgiving.

There are other ways you can help out in your community, and the weeks just before Thanksgiving might be just the time to show your appreciation for the town or neighborhood you live in. Is there a place where kids play that's gotten a little run-down? If so, maybe a group of you could get together and spend an hour or two cleaning up. Take trash bags and twist ties with you to hold litter and discarded bottles and cans. Be very careful if you are picking up broken glass. It's a good idea to put the jagged pieces in a sturdy brown paper sack so they won't cut through the plastic trash bag. If there are graffiti on a wall, why not ask the owner of the property if he or she would like help painting it over? You could supply the labor and the owner could supply the paint and brushes.

How about moving your clean-up operation to your own yard? Your parents will be thrilled to have the last of the leaves raked and bagged or the firewood neatly stacked. If you live in a warm climate, you probably have outdoor furniture that could use a wash before the holiday.

As you are tidying up the yard, keep your eyes peeled for twigs and sticks that would make good kindling. A paper shopping bag full of these small pieces of wood with a ribbon tying the handles together makes a terrific thank-you gift for that neighbor who fixed your bike or helped you with your homework. And, of course, if your own house has a fireplace, a sack of kindling will be a swell surprise for whoever lights the fire.

17

Don't the birds deserve a Thanksgiving dinner, too? Fill the feeder in your backyard or make a simple treat for them. Find a good-sized fallen pine cone and loop some string or fishing line under the first layer of scales for a hanger. Then spread peanut butter all over the cone, making sure it gets packed into the spaces, and tie the feeder to a tree limb. Before you know it, the small birds will be busily eating their treat.

There is another easy way to make a bird feeder. You'll need a mesh bag like the kind onions are packaged in and a lump of suet from the butcher. Suet, which is a kind of animal fat, is usually thrown away, so most butchers are happy to give you some for free. Cut open the bag and snip out a piece of mesh about ten inches square. Put the suet in the middle of it, draw up the corners to meet, and tie it with string to make a little package. This feeder, too, can be hung by string or fishing line from a tree limb and will attract lots of eager eaters.

Another way to share the Thanksgiving spirit is just to say thanks to people who've been especially kind or helpful. But instead of simply saying it in person, why not announce it to the world? Make a "thank you" board!

This is a good group project to do at school, Sunday school, the library, or even town hall. You need either some space on a bulletin board in one of these buildings or permission to hang a "board" of your own. A sheet of poster board or even a large piece of cardboard painted an attractive color will do fine.

Your "thank you" board probably needs a title to let people know what it's all about. Some possibilities are: WE WANT TO THANK YOU, THE THANKS-GIVING CENTER, or simply THE THANKS BOARD. You can cut letters out of construction paper or write on a long paper strip in felt-tip pen and then stick it across the top of the board.

Get things started yourself. If your thanks board is at school, you probably have a teacher you're especially fond of. Write your thanks note on a small piece of paper and tape or tack it to the board. "Thanks, Mrs. Jensen—At last I understand math!" or "Thanks to Mr. March for taking us on the best field trip ever" are the kind of thing you might write. And don't forget some of the people you see less often, like the school nurse or the principal's secretary or the janitor who let you back into the classroom when you left your best sweater in your desk.

The members of your group who put up the thanks board will be prepared with their own thanks notes to tack on it. But here's a suggestion to help out people who walk by and see it and want to add a note themselves. Put a sign on the board saying WANT TO THANK SOMEONE? Then attach a pad and pencil to the board with string for instant notes. And be sure to leave extra tape or tacks. It will be fun for everyone to read the nice things people have said about them.

It's pretty obvious that a thanks board in school will have notes to teachers and other people who work there. But a board at Sunday school could thank members of the congregation as well. And one in the library or town hall might thank anyone in the community. You could even make a thanks board for your home. Wouldn't your brothers and sisters like to know how much you appreciate them? And how about other family members? Parents and grandparents and aunts and uncles all will feel good when they read thanks notes dedicated to them. And maybe you'll even find a note or two on the board meant for you!

David —
Thanks for teaching me
to skate backward!
Susan

What's the best dance to do on
Thanksgiving?

The Turkey Trot.

Can a turkey fly higher than the Empire State
Building?

Yes. The Empire State Building can't fly at all.

3. Thanksgiving Across the Miles

Thanksgiving is traditionally a holiday when family members gather, but what about the relatives who can't be there? Even if they are having a happy turkey feast with friends, these aunts and uncles and grandparents still need to know that they are missed by you and your family.

One way to tell your out-of-town relatives that you are thinking of them is with a card. But don't just buy a card at the store. The simplest one you make yourself will mean more to them than the most glamorous and expensive card found in a shop.

23

You don't have to think up a whole long flowery poem or write them a three-page letter. A short phrase like "Thanks for being the best grandma in the world" or "Wish you were here to spend Thanksgiving with us" says it all.

Especially for family members who haven't seen you in quite a while, it's nice to include a recent snapshot of yourself. If you haven't gotten this year's school pictures yet and you think last year's were really horrible, why not ask Mom or Dad if there's an extra photo from your summer trip that you can send with your note? Or you might decide to draw a self-portrait and paste it on your card.

Funny cards are always a success. Use a great Thanksgiving joke or riddle to cheer up your grandma who isn't able to be with you for the holiday. You'll find a number of possibilities in this book if you can't come up with one of your own.

Of course, you can make your card as fancy as you want, but here's a suggestion for one that's quick and easy to do. Take a sheet of construction paper or regular typing paper and fold it into thirds, like a letter. On the front of the top flap write or print the first part of your riddle or joke. Put the answer on the front of the bottom flap and add a little smile face to show that you're teasing. Now there is plenty of room on the inside for your message and your photo or self-portrait. And don't forget to sign your name!

Make sure to send your Thanksgiving card a few days before

25

the holiday so it will be received in time. Remember that there is no mail delivery on Thanksgiving Day.

Another wonderful gift for faraway family members is a Thanksgiving tape. Most people spend part of the holiday calling friends and relatives long distance. But with everyone crowded around the phone and someone reminding you that long-distance calls cost money, it's hard to say more than hello and goodbye. With a taped message all of you have time to say as much as you want. And since the tape recorder can be turned off and on and rewound to tape over something, you can make sure your message says just what you want it to.

Of course, a tape made by the whole crowd on Thanksgiving Day won't be received until a couple of days later, but it's a permanent reminder of the whole family's loving thoughts that can be played over and over. Everyone will be pleased and impressed that you came up with this idea and got things organized to carry it out.

All you really need is a tape recorder and a blank cassette. Be sure that the batteries are fresh—it's a good idea to have a set of extras just in case. If the recorder is a plug-in type, figure out where you can use it without getting in the way of all the dinner preparations. And if there is a separate microphone, check to make sure it works. In fact, you will want to do a short test taping a day or two before Thanksgiving to try out the recorder and practice speaking into it.

You are going to be the "talk show host" for your Thanksgiving tape. This means that you will speak first, giving a short introduction, and then identify each new person on tape before he or she talks. (Remember that it isn't always easy to recognize people's voices on tape.) Your advance test taping is a good chance to rehearse what you plan to say. Then you'll have time to change it if you don't like the way it sounds.

It's a smart move to write out your introductory remarks, especially if you feel nervous about talking into a microphone or are afraid you'll forget what you were going to say. Somewhere near the beginning you'll want to give some specific information like your name, the date, the place where the tape is being made, and probably the names of the people who are present, including any babies who won't be speaking into the recorder. You could say something like this:

"Hi, Grandma and Grandpa. This is Suzie, speaking to you from our house in Springfield. It's Thanksgiving Day, 1987, and we all wish you were here with us. Aunt Joan and Uncle Bob arrived last night and the whole Johnson gang got here this morning—Aunt Debbie, Uncle Chad, and Ricky, Jill, and Mikey. Of course Grandma Morris is out in the kitchen helping Mom, and Mary Lou came home from college and brought her roommate, Sara, with her. Brownie and Whiskers are here, too, but they're not going to say anything, I hope! Now Dad's going to talk first. Here he is."

28

You may wonder how you could know the day before that Grandma Morris would be out in the kitchen helping your mom when you started talking on the tape. The answer is, of course, that you don't. But putting in some information about what people are doing as the tape is being made gives the listener a feeling of being there with you. And you can easily change the script to tell what's actually happening. Maybe your grandma will be giving little Mikey his bottle when you start the tape, and so you'll say that instead.

Since you are the host of this taped family "talk show," it's your job to make sure it goes smoothly. Be alert for glitches —someone dropping the microphone or getting a sneezing fit in the middle of a sentence makes a lot of unpleasant noise on the tape. The way to fix this is to rewind the tape—probably to the place where that person started speaking—and begin again. You may want to replay each person's segment to make sure that it's loud enough before moving on. And, of course, you'll be the one to monitor the tape and change it over to the other side when it runs out.

Although you want to keep background noise to a minimum, you don't want this tape to sound as if it were made on the moon instead of in your own home. When the dog starts barking frantically because your big sister and her roommate are about to take him for a walk, why not explain that on the tape instead of erasing it? Your grandparents will feel as if they are

part of what's going on, and Grandpa will remember taking Brownie for walks when he was visiting.

Take advantage of the unexpected. If your dad and uncle start yelling at the TV, take the microphone and say, "Hear that deafening noise? It's only Dad and Uncle Bob cheering because the home team just scored a touchdown. Hope you saw that one, Grandpa. And now back to Aunt Debbie."

Once everyone has had a chance to talk on the tape, finish your "talk show" with some kind of short wrap-up. Something like "Well, that's the way it is for this Thanksgiving. Goodbye for now. And Happy Thanksgiving from all of us" will work fine. But you might want to give Grandma and Grandpa a chuckle. You could tell a joke or a riddle or even recite a short silly poem. Here's one that's been around for years.

> A turkey is a funny bird,
> Its head goes wobble, wobble.
> All it knows is just one word,
> "Gobble, gobble, gobble."

And if you can get everyone to yell "Happy Thanksgiving!" at the very end of the tape, that will be great.

Mail the tape in a padded envelope or wrap it in a couple of pieces of newspaper and put it in a small manila envelope. And get ready for a repeat performance next year. This is a Thanksgiving tradition that's sure to be a big hit!

What do you get when you cross a turkey
with an octopus?

Enough drumsticks for Thanksgiving.

How can you make a turkey float?

You need two scoops of ice cream,
some root beer,
and a turkey.

4. Food for the Holiday Table

Part of the fun of Thanksgiving is getting everything ready. The aroma of roasting turkey and the sight of glistening red cranberry sauce say Thanksgiving to almost everyone in this country. Food is the focal point of this holiday.

Isn't it amazing that families sit down to pretty much the same Thanksgiving dinner year after year and no one seems to get tired of it? Most of the menu is very traditional. Who would think of Thanksgiving without turkey? And, of course, there are cranberries, cornbread stuffing, sweet potatoes, and pumpkin pie. Though there may be additions and variations, this basic holiday dinner has been served all over the United States for generations.

Why these foods and not others? Why not peach pie instead of pumpkin, or roast beef instead of turkey? The most likely explanation is that most Thanksgiving foods are native to North America. Flocks of wild turkeys, as well as ducks and geese, lived in the woodlands of the northeast. The tangy cranberries used to flavor most Thanksgiving meals grew wild in the New England bogs. And the Indians who helped the Pilgrims survive in the New World showed them how to grow corn, beans, and pumpkins. The first Thanksgivings were celebrating successful harvests, using the crops that were grown here and the wild foods that were available.

These days, of course, foods that didn't originate here are found on the holiday table, along with others that the Pilgrims had never heard of. They certainly didn't have marshmallow-topped sweet potatoes or Jell-O for molded salads.

But it's fun to have some of the traditional foods prepared in new ways. Here are several tasty treats you can make ahead of time as your contribution to an old-fashioned Thanksgiving dinner.

TANGY CRANBERRY RELISH

Why not make your own cranberry sauce with real cranberries? This flavorful variation keeps well in the refrigerator, so you can make it several days in advance. It's so easy to do and so delicious that making it might become a new Thanksgiving tradition at your house.

You need:

- a food processor or a blender (be sure you have an adult's permission or adult help), or a food grinder
- 1 12-ounce bag of raw cranberries (found in the produce section of the market)
- 2 medium oranges
- 1/2 to 1 cup of sugar

35

How to do it:

Rinse the cranberries and throw out any really soft ones. Wash the oranges and remove any stem. With an adult's permission or adult help, cut the oranges into eighths. Leave the peel on but get rid of the seeds.

Grind the cranberries and oranges together. Do only half at a time so all the fruit gets evenly chopped. Be very careful when using a food processor or blender, and run it in short bursts so the relish doesn't turn into mush.

Put the cranberry-orange mixture in a bowl and add a half cup of sugar. Stir it thoroughly and taste it. If it's too tart, add more sugar, a quarter cup at a time, until it tastes good. Remember, it shouldn't be too sweet.

Dump the cranberry relish into a covered container and put it in the refrigerator until serving time. This recipe makes enough relish for 10–12 people.

CRANBERRY SURPRISE PIE

Cranberries are always part of Thanksgiving, but why restrict them to sauce for the turkey? Let them take on a new role as part of this sweet and colorful dessert. Whichever variation you choose, you're sure to get lots of compliments. But be careful—these pies may be so popular that you'll have to make them every year!

You need:
- 1 quart of vanilla ice cream *or* orange sherbet
- 1 cup canned whole-berry cranberry sauce
- 1 store-bought or homemade graham cracker pie crust *or* 8 individual mini pie crusts

How to do it:
Scoop all the ice cream or sherbet into a bowl and add the cranberry sauce. Mush it all together with a large spoon until

37

it's fairly evenly mixed. Work quickly so that the ice cream or sherbet doesn't get too runny.

Spoon the mixture into the pie crust and smooth it into an attractive shape. Put the pie into the freezer to harden for at least an hour. Or make the pie a day or two in advance and keep it in the freezer till serving time. This dessert serves 8 people.

PUMPKIN ICE CREAM PIE

Of course, regular pumpkin pie is a traditional part of the menu, but there is often someone who doesn't really like it. This variation on the cranberry pie is a terrific crowd-pleaser and is "easy as pie" to put together.

You need:

- 1 cup of plain canned pumpkin (not pumpkin pie filling)
- 1/4 cup of sugar
- 1/2 teaspoon of pumpkin pie spice *or* 1/4 teaspoon each of cinnamon and ginger
- 1 quart of vanilla ice cream
- 1 store-bought or homemade graham cracker pie crust *or* 8 individual mini pie crusts

Optional:
- whipped cream
- walnut or pecan halves

How to do it:

Make this the same way as the Cranberry Surprise Pie. Mix the pumpkin, sugar, and spices together and then add the ice cream. Mush it together and remember to work fast so the ice cream doesn't get runny.

Spoon the ice cream mixture into the pie crust and smooth it with the back of the spoon so it looks nice. Then quickly put the pie into the freezer to harden.

If you are using the whipped cream and nut halves, add them in a decorative ring around the edge of the pie before serving. This dessert serves 8 people.

FROSTY GINGERBREAD

Gingerbread fits right in with an old-fashioned Thanksgiving. Cake-type gingerbread has been a favorite dessert for generations. And since the flavor of ginger goes so well with pumpkin, this easy-to-make ice cream cake is a perfect ending to your holiday meal. If you know someone who was born around Thanksgiving, try this cake as a wonderful birthday surprise.

You need:

- 2 round cake pans
- 1 package of gingerbread mix
- 1 cup of plain canned pumpkin (not pumpkin pie filling)
- 1/4 cup of sugar
- 1/4 teaspoon of cinnamon
- 1/4 teaspoon of nutmeg
- 1 quart of vanilla ice cream

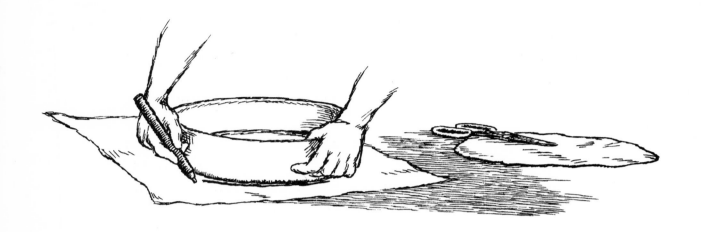

How to do it:

Make the gingerbread batter according to the directions on the box. Grease the sides of both cake pans. If you have spring-form cake pans (the kind with sides that come off), use those. If not, you'll need to line the bottom of your pans with paper. You can use either waxed paper or brown wrapping paper, but do not use plastic wrap. Trace around the pans (felt-tip pen shows up best on waxed paper), and after cutting out the paper circles, place one in the bottom of each pan.

Make sure you have an adult's permission or adult help when lighting and using the oven. Pour half the batter into each pan and bake according to the directions on the box. (Be very careful with the hot oven and remember to use pot holders.) Since your gingerbread cakes are thinner than usual, they will need less baking time than the package calls for. The directions on the box explain how to tell when the gingerbread is done; check it when there's still ten minutes to go.

When the cakes are done, let them cool completely in the pans.

Once the cakes are cool, you're ready for the ice cream topping. In a large bowl mix the pumpkin, sugar, and spices. Add the ice cream and mush it all together until it's fairly evenly mixed. Work quickly so the ice cream doesn't get runny.

Spread half the ice cream mixture in each pan, on top of the gingerbread. Put the pans into the freezer for at least an hour to let the ice cream harden.

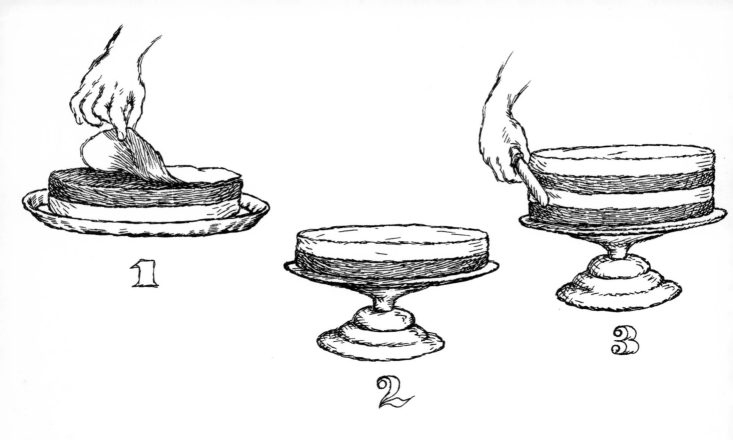

When you are ready to serve dessert, take the pans out and run a table knife around the edge of each to loosen the sides. If you've used spring-form pans, take off the sides and the bottoms. If not, turn each pan over on top of a plate, rap it with your knuckles, and gently lift the pan off the cake. Peel the waxed paper off the bottoms of both cakes.

44

Flip one cake over onto the serving plate so that the ice cream is on top. Flatten and smooth the ice cream with a table knife if necessary. Then carefully turn over the other cake and set it on top of the first one, ice cream side on top. Smooth the ice cream along the sides so that the cake looks neat and pretty. Now you have a four-layer pumpkin-ginger ice cream cake that will impress everyone! This dessert serves 12 people.

What kind of music did the Pilgrims like best?

Plymouth Rock.

Which side of a turkey has the most feathers?

The outside.

5. Start Some New Traditions

Have you just had a fight with your sister or are you mad at your dad because his rules seem too strict? All of us get upset with our families from time to time. It's perfectly normal. But when you stop and think about your family and your home, you realize there's a lot to be thankful for.

Now is a good time to show your family how important they are to you. You can make something for all of them to enjoy during the holiday.

47

Harvest Home Centerpiece

If your family doesn't have a centerpiece that's always on the Thanksgiving table, why not make one? Bring back the memories of harvest home with a table decoration made out of some of nature's bounty. This centerpiece is a handy size and will fit on a coffee table or sideboard if the dining-room table is too loaded with food. The Styrofoam base gives the wreath a nice three-dimensional look.

You need:

- a Styrofoam ring—either buy one in an 8- to 10-inch size or tape together 2 large Styrofoam plates and cut out the center
- small natural materials—gather up such things as colorful fallen leaves, nuts, acorns, dry seed pods, small pine cones, dried flower heads, berries, crab apples, or things from the kitchen like pumpkin seeds, curly parsley, carrot tops, a small head of garlic
- white glue

How to do it:

First arrange the materials you've found on the Styrofoam ring until you're happy with the look. You might want to start with the colorful leaves, arranging them to cover the ring, and then add the berries and seed pods and other bits in groups on top. Or you might like the more uniform look of neat rows of nuts alternating with pine cones and berries.

Once you're satisfied with the arrangement, glue everything in place. The white glue will dry clear, so don't be afraid to use as much as you need. Let your wreath dry thoroughly before you move it.

Optional additions:

A mound of small gourds and fruits inside the ring adds to the feeling of bountiful harvest. Look for interesting colors and shapes. Try things like tiny pumpkins or acorn squash, ornamental squash, Indian corn, small tangerines and apples, grapes, lemons, or limes. You might decide on an autumn harvest arrangement of gourds, nuts, and apples, or you might prefer a selection of just fruit. You can rearrange this mound in the center of the wreath until you're pleased with it, but be careful not to pile things so high that they'll roll away when someone bumps the table.

CANDLED APPLES

These apple candleholders are a dramatic addition to any Thanksgiving table and are easy and inexpensive to make. But before you decide to make them, check with Mom or Dad to be sure there'll be a place to put lit candles. They can be arranged either inside or outside the wreath centerpiece or stand by themselves on a table.

You need:

- apple corer
- 2 or more large Rome Beauty apples that stand firmly and evenly on a flat surface
- the same number of candles
- small plates, coasters, or rounds of aluminum foil to catch drips

How to do it:

Using the apple corer, make a hole about halfway through the center of each apple from the top; work carefully so you don't cut your fingers. Try to make the hole as straight up and down as possible so that your candle won't stand at an angle. The corer will make a hole about the right size for a regular candle, and if the hole is a little small, that's fine. The candle will have a nice tight fit.

Stick the candles into the apples. If a hole is a little too big and your candle feels loose, wrap the bottom end of the candle with some waxed paper or tissue for a better fit. If a hole is too crooked to fix, save this apple for Thanksgiving Day breakfast (see page 62), and start over with another apple.

Place the candlesticks where they will look best. Once you're happy with the arrangement, put a circle of foil or a saucer under each one to protect the table and the tablecloth.

"THANKS A LOT" NAPKIN RINGS

Everyone at the dinner table will feel welcome and appreciated with these dual-purpose personalized place card–napkin rings. There will be no doubt about who sits where, and the whole gang will love taking turns reading their very own secret messages.

This is a great project for you to share with your brothers and sisters and cousins. Divide up the names of everyone who'll be there for Thanksgiving dinner, and you can all help one another think of just the right way to say thanks.

You need:

- pencil, ruler, and scissors
- construction paper in a color that goes with the table decor
- felt-tip pens in a color that will show up on the construction paper

How to do it:

Draw a 6-inch by 1 1/2-inch rectangle on the construction paper and cut it out. Snip a slit a little more than halfway up, about 1/2 inch in from each end (see diagram). Slide the ends together to form the napkin ring. Try it on one of the napkins that will be used for Thanksgiving dinner to make sure it's

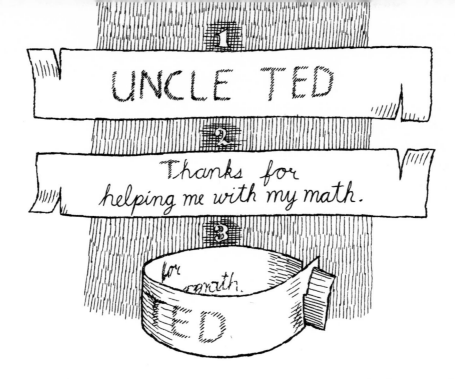

large enough. Adjust the size if necessary and then make enough napkin rings for everyone.

In large letters neatly print one name on each napkin ring. Then turn the napkin rings over and fill in the secret thank-you messages. "Thanks for teaching me to knit. Love, Kathy" or "I love your chocolate cake and I love you. Thanks from Bill" are short enough to fit and say what you want them to. If someone you don't know very well is coming for dinner, you can say something like "Thanks for being with us on Thanksgiving." Whatever you say will be a nice surprise as people sit down at the table.

LIVING FAMILY TREE

This is a wonderful project for you to start and for your family members to help with. It's amazing to see how the "branches" of your family spread out, even if you are an only child. As relatives add names to the tree, you'll probably find out about cousins you've never heard of before.

Ask your grandparents or aunts and uncles to tell you more about these newly discovered members of the family. Once you get them started, you'll find they have lots to say. Hearing about the way things were before you were born is fascinating. It's as much fun for Grandpa to tell about being a soldier in World War II as it is for you to hear it. And your aunt's humorous description of how she learned to drive a tractor will have everyone laughing.

Talking about the history of your family helps make everyone feel closer. It gives you all an opportunity to be thankful for being a part of this interesting bunch of people. And this is a tradition the whole family will want to continue.

You need:
- a roll of plain white shelf paper
- a Post-it note pad (the 3″ × 3″ size)
- pens, pencils, scissors, and a ruler

How to do it:

A day or two before Thanksgiving get out the shelf paper and Post-its and begin your family tree. Cut about a yard of shelf paper from the roll and lay it flat. (You may need more later, but this is a good size to start with.) Tear off a few Post-it pages and cut them in half so that both halves have sticky stuff on one end. These will be the name tags for your family tree.

On the first name tag write your full name and birthdate. Stick the tag on the shelf paper next to the bottom edge and near the middle. Do you have brothers or sisters? If so, put their full names and birthdates on separate name tags and line them up on the shelf paper next to yours. This lowest level of the family tree is the generation you and your brothers and sisters and your first cousins all belong to.

Make name tags for your mom and dad, with their birthdates if you know them. Put them close together centered above you and your brothers and sisters. This is the next generation older than yours.

Do you know if your mom and dad have any brothers or sisters? These people would be your aunts and uncles. Make tags for whichever ones you're sure about and put them next to Mom or Dad. If they are married and have children, put in tags for the wives and husbands on that generational level and for the children, your first cousins, on the same generational level as your tag. (Now you can see why the Post-it tags are so useful. You've probably already moved several tags around to make room for everybody.)

The next generation up is, of course, your grandparents and their brothers and sisters. You will probably need help to fill in this line. For now just fill in your grandmother and grandfather on each side. When everyone shows up on Thanksgiving Day, you'll be able to add more details.

If members of your family have been divorced or widowed and remarried, this adds complications to your family tree. You may have half-sisters and brothers or step-sisters and brothers. There may be other people who aren't actually related to you by blood but are very much members of your family. Look at the sample family trees on pages 58–59 to see some ways of arranging your own. Remember that you can add more paper to the sides or even to the bottom or top of the tree whenever you need it.

Take advantage of the natural lulls before and after Thanksgiving dinner to spread out your family tree and get help on filling in the missing pieces. You'll find that almost everyone has something to say, and you can add interesting tidbits like "stowed away on boat to US" or "ran for mayor in 1938" to some of the tags.

When your family tree is as complete as possible and you've arranged the tags neatly in their generational patterns, you can draw in the equal signs (=) for marriages and the lines from parents to children. A slash line through the equal sign indicates divorce.

You'll want to save your family tree for next year. Maybe by then someone will have remembered the name of that distant cousin or whatever happened to Great-aunt Mathilda. In order to preserve all your hard work, be sure to tape down the name tags or remove them and draw in boxes on the shelf paper in their place. Then you can roll up the family tree and put it away without worrying that the tags will come off.

When your cousins see this family tree, they'll probably want to do their own. One side of theirs, of course, will be the same as one side of yours, but the other half will show the members of another whole family group. Next Thanksgiving you can line up these family trees and see where they connect.

But you don't need to wait a whole year to work on family trees. Any family gathering is a good opportunity to talk over old times and renew the sense of belonging that family ties create.

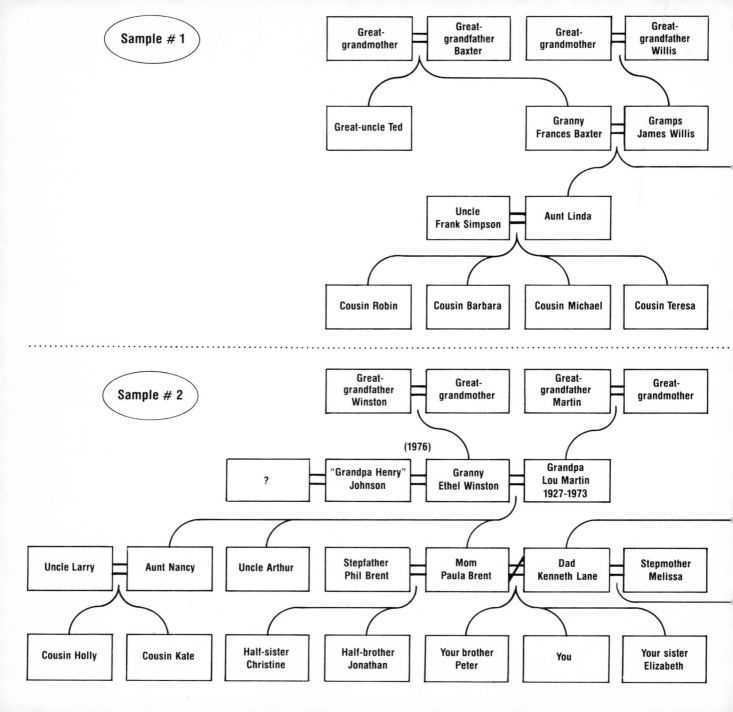

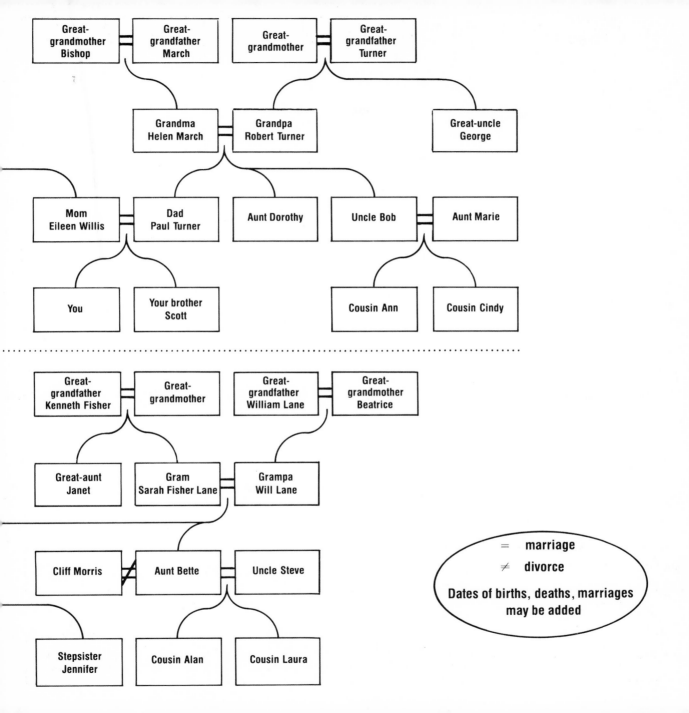

Why did they let the turkey join the band?

It had drumsticks.

Why did the police arrest the turkey?

They suspected it of fowl play.

6. A Special Beginning

The day of Thanksgiving itself is full of activity. It seems there's always something that needs to be done—setting the table, putting out the good glasses and napkins, finding a place for people to put their coats and boots, keeping the dog from eating the cheese ball on the coffee table.

Since the holiday meal is usually earlier than regular dinner and the kitchen is swamped all day with food preparations, lunch may be pretty skimpy. All the more reason for a hearty breakfast to start things off. Your whole family will thank you

61

for your thoughtfulness when you serve them this deliciously different morning menu.

THANKSGIVING DAY BREAKFAST
Orange juice or other fruit juice
Baked Apples
Cranberry Corn Muffins
Filled Crescent Rolls
Milk; coffee or tea

All the food but the Filled Crescent Rolls can be made the evening or day before so you won't be in a mad rush in the morning and can sit down and enjoy breakfast with everyone else. Why not set the table right before you go to bed on Wednesday night, and then breakfast will really be a snap!

BAKED APPLES

These are often served as dessert, but there's no reason to reserve them for the evening. Baked apples can be a tasty and healthful morning fruit. Serve them cold, or in wintry weather heat them for a few minutes in the oven. Some people like to pour milk or cream over them, so you might want to put a small pitcher of milk or cream on the table.

You need:

- apple corer, baking pan
- 1 apple per person—nice fat Rome Beauties work well, as do any cooking apples
- some brown sugar, cinnamon, and butter or margarine

Optional:
- raisins

How to do it:

Wash the apples and core them all the way through so there aren't any seeds left inside or any stem on either end (be careful when using the apple corer). Stand the apples in the baking pan; don't worry if they're crowded. Pour in some water until it's about a half inch deep.

Now you are ready to add the flavorings to the empty apple

centers. If you are using raisins, put them in the holes first, about a heaping teaspoon per apple. You don't need to measure the butter. Just put a little lump of it, about the size of a jelly bean or marble, on the tip of a knife and scrape it into each apple. Next pour between a half and a whole teaspoon of sugar (if you don't have brown, use white) into each apple. Add a small shake of cinnamon to each apple center, and you're ready to put the pan into the oven. You should have an adult's permission or adult help when lighting and using the oven. Be sure to use pot holders. Bake the apples for about an hour at 375° F.

CRANBERRY CORN MUFFINS

If you like corn muffins, you'll love these! They are a special Thanksgiving variation, but you might want to have them for Sunday breakfasts all the time once you've seen how easy they are to make and how good they taste.

You need:

- muffin tins and paper muffin liners
- 1 package of corn muffin mix
- whatever the mix calls for, usually milk and an egg
- 1 cup of canned whole-berry cranberry sauce

How to do it:

Prepare the muffin mix according to package directions. Then stir in the cranberry sauce; you don't need to stir it very much.

Put the papers in the tins and then fill them about half to two-thirds full. (You may need one or two more papers and tin spaces than the package calls for because you are adding the cranberry sauce.) You should have an adult's permission or adult help when lighting or using the oven. Follow the package instructions for baking.

FILLED CRESCENT ROLLS

These hearty main-dish rolls can be filled with a variety of meats and cheeses. Use whatever your family especially likes. The rolls are quick and easy to put together but do need to bake in the oven for fifteen to twenty minutes. Make two for each person and have some more ready to pop into the oven. They'll disappear fast! And they do taste a lot better when they're freshly baked, so don't make them the night before.

You need:
· cookie sheets and a spatula
· refrigerated tubes of crescent dinner rolls—
  enough for at least 2 rolls per person

- sliced cheese, such as cheddar, Monterey jack, Swiss, mozzarella, or whatever your family likes—about 1/2 slice per roll
- thin-sliced cooked meats, such as bologna, ham, turkey, or roast beef (slices must be thin enough to roll up)—about the same amount as the cheese

How to do it:

Open the tubes of crescent rolls. This may be a little difficult, but follow the package directions and use the edge of a spoon to split the seam if it doesn't just pop open. Now unroll the dough and carefully separate the triangles at the perforations.

Place a slice of cheese and a slice of meat on one triangle. Don't worry if the edges of the fillings hang out a bit. Roll up the dough triangle starting from the wide end, and then put it on the cookie sheet with the point on the bottom so it doesn't unroll. You won't be able to bend these filled rolls into crescent shapes the way the package says.

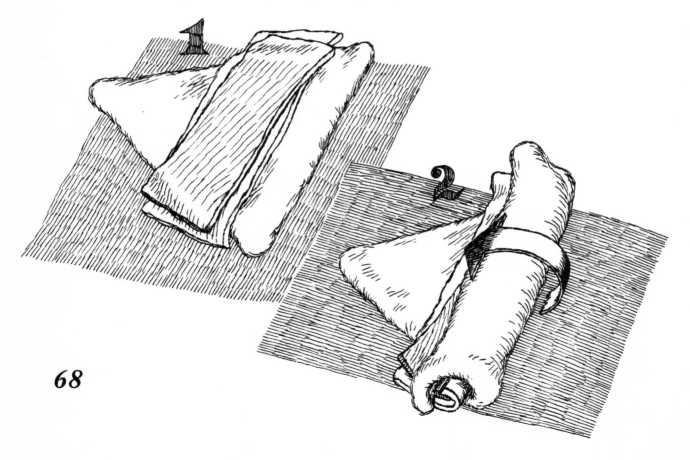

Continue until you've filled as many triangles as you need. Be sure to have an adult's permission or adult help when lighting and using the oven. Bake the first batch according to the package directions, but add two or three minutes to the baking time. Of course, use caution and pot holders around the hot oven. While the rolls are baking, call everyone to the table so the rolls can be served piping hot.

Luckily there's not much to clean up after this great simple breakfast. Just be sure to put the dishes away after you wash them so there's room for the turkey preparations.

Making this breakfast is a terrific way for you and your brothers and sisters to show Mom and Dad how much you appreciate them. The kids preparing Thanksgiving breakfast for the grown-ups is likely to become a holiday tradition that everyone looks forward to.

What's the key to a great Thanksgiving
dinner?

The tur-key.

What did the turkey say before it was
roasted?

"Wow, I'm stuffed!"

7. Giving Thanks Together

This is what Thanksgiving is all about: family and friends gathered from near and far, the aroma of roasting turkey coming from the kitchen, a feeling of warmth and good cheer spreading through the house.

The kitchen is the hub of activity for most of the day. You've saved yourself one last food surprise to prepare now, so that you can be where the action is. It's fun to have a project of your own to do, and you won't feel as if you're in anyone's way as you put together this simple recipe.

DOUBLE-CHEESE CHEESE BALL

This is the perfect way to take the edge off everyone's hunger during the last hour before dinner. It's a light yet tasty appetizer that combines the flavors and textures of two different cheeses. Serve it on a plate surrounded by crackers, or provide celery sticks to spread it on for a great crunchy-creamy contrast.

You need:

- 4 ounces of grated cheddar cheese—you can grate it yourself if you want to
- 1 8-ounce container of soft cream cheese—not the whipped kind

How to do it:

Use a fork to mix half of the grated cheddar cheese with all of the soft cream cheese in a bowl. When it's fairly evenly mixed, you are ready to make the cheese ball.

Spread out the rest of the grated cheese on a plate or piece of waxed paper. You are going to roll the cheese ball in it. Also get out the plate you are going to serve the finished cheese ball on. Once you start making the cheese ball, your hands will be too messy to touch anything!

Now scrape all the cheese mixture into a lump in your hand. You'll need to use a rubber scraper or spoon to get it all out of the bowl. With both hands pat the cheese mixture into a ball the same way you make a snowball.

When it's nice and round, roll it in the rest of the grated cheddar to give it a hairy orange coat. Don't worry if some of the grated cheddar doesn't stick to the cheese ball. Just gather up as much as you can and then put your cheese ball on the middle of the serving plate. Surround it with crackers or celery

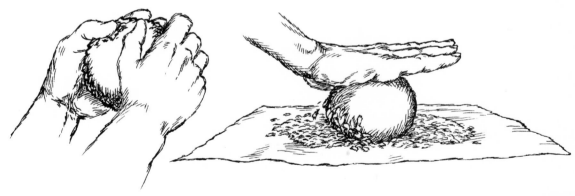

sticks, and you're all set! If it's not time for hors d'oeuvres yet, put your cheese ball (on its plate) into the refrigerator without the crackers.

The cheese ball tastes great without anything else added, but for extra zing you can mix in a little (about 1/2 teaspoon) mustard. Or you can have an herbal ball by adding a teaspoon of chopped chives and a shake or two of paprika.

When everybody is ready for a before-dinner snack, bring out your cheese ball and put it on the coffee table. You might also want to make a plate of apple slices and celery sticks spread with peanut butter and take that out, too. You may be amazed at how quickly everything disappears!

A Photo Opportunity

This time before dinner—when everything is ready but the turkey—is the perfect opportunity for a group project. Does your family have a whole box of snapshots from various trips and holiday gatherings that have never been sorted out? Many families have a bunch of photos that someone has planned to put into an album but never got around to. Why not get started now?

If you have an album all ready to be filled, that's great. But if not, you can still sort and label the photos and get rid of the ones that are totally out of focus. It's fun to look over these snapshots and remember where you all were and what you were doing.

While the whole gang is right there in your living room, you can help one another recall names and places. Grandpa may be the only person who remembers the name of that man who helped you catch tadpoles in the lake last summer. And your little sister might surprise you all by recognizing the tree that marked the edge of the campground you all visited last fall. Don't forget to take a couple of group shots now to be added to the album later on.

Whether you are filling up the family album or simply identifying people and places, be sure to have the necessary tools available, such as a felt-tip pen to mark the photos with or little slips of paper to label the album pages. And give the writing assignment to someone else because you have another important job to do.

How about having a lottery to decide who's going to do which job to help with dinner? That way everyone will get to do something, but it will be sort of like a game. Talk this over in advance with Mom or Dad, and make out a list of what things need to be done.

Even though the table may already be set, you can think of an amazing number of ways to help once you get going. How about:

- filling the water glasses
- putting the refrigerated items like butter, cranberry sauce, and the relish tray out on the table
- refilling the gravy boat
- clearing the dinner plates
- throwing away the bones so the dog doesn't get them
- bringing in the dessert plates
- bringing in the cups and saucers
- making sure the cream and sugar are on the table

You'll no doubt think of other jobs. There's always plenty to do in serving a holiday dinner. Just make sure that you have the same number of jobs as guests. And if there are young children who will want to help, figure out chores that are safe for them to do.

Once you've got your list, it's easy to put the lottery together. Write each job on a separate slip of paper and fold the papers closed. Get a hat or some other container to hold your lottery slips. Shortly before dinner is to be served, pass the hat and let Fate decide who does what. (However, mark the supereasy job slips with an X and make sure the little kids pick those.)

Everyone will be delighted to take part in your lottery. People always want to help, but sometimes it's hard to know what kind of help will be appreciated. It's so much easier to have an assigned job in advance. This is one idea that's bound to become an instant Thanksgiving tradition.

LINKED HANDS

Dinner is announced and you all move toward the dining-room table. Some people detour through the kitchen to carry out the jobs they've picked. Others mill around the table, reading the placemark napkin rings and figuring out where they're supposed to sit.

Soon the bowls of steaming vegetables have been placed on the table and the turkey is carried in. Your mouth is watering as you look forward to that first delicious bite.

But before the person at the head of the table starts carving up the bird, you all join hands to give thanks for this food and for other things in your lives. As you go around the table, each person telling what he or she is most thankful for, you wonder what you'll say when it's your turn.

As you try to decide, you realize that there are so many things you are thankful for. Some of them are when hard work paid off, like doing well on your spelling test or getting that Scout merit badge in record time. Some were sort of lucky breaks, like getting the teacher you really wanted this year. Or what about when the skateboard you were dying to have went on sale and Dad bought it for you? And some things come from just thinking about your family and friends and knowing that they are very special to you.

You feel the clasp of friendly hands in yours. Looking around the table, you see those faces that make you feel so good. And then you hear someone take the words right out of your mouth: "I'm thankful for this most wonderful Thanksgiving ever."

INDEX